Light
Inspired

Jennifer Pang

Balboa Press books may be ordered through booksellers or by contacting:

Balboa Press
A Division of Hay House
1663 Liberty Drive
Bloomington, IN 47403
www.balboapress.com
844-682-1282

ISBN: 979-8-7652-4751-8 (sc)
ISBN: 979-8-7652-4752-5 (hc)
ISBN: 979-8-7652-4750-1 (e)

Library of Congress Control Number: 2023922260

Print information available on the last page.

Balboa Press rev. date: 11/22/2023

Your word is a lamp for my feet, a light on my path

Psalm 119:105

1

My life got too loud
God was trying to speak to me
I could not hear Him

In faith I stepped out
In stillness He spoke to me
His voice a whisper

Allow for stillness
Banish noise, quiet your mind
Sit, breathe, and just be

Find in your stillness
A connection with your soul
Noise fades and peace reigns

Avoid life conformed
Deep abiding peace your guide
Surrender your fears

Filled with angst and doubt
Love God more and worry less
Strength and peace be found

Live in hope and faith
Travel the road less travelled
Your life unscripted

Gifted with free will
In His infinite goodness
Choose the life you want

Often said, "One day…"
We postpone our hopes and dreams
Expecting more time

Taken for granted
Tomorrows are not assured
"One day" is today

Carpe diem!!!

When at a crossroad
Prayer is the place to start
Seek out His guidance

That small voice inside
The guidance of divine grace
Your compass, true north

Season of waiting
Impatient to know the end
Be still and abide

In the wait, prepare
Make ready for what's to come
All in divine time

In this new season
Leave behind what does not serve
Move forth unburdened

Daily mindfulness
Live your life with intention
Life with joy and peace

Light in the darkness
Be a spark that ignites change
The world is waiting

In you resides hope
You are the light of the world
Go forth and shine bright

Sow the seeds of faith
Acts of kindness to strangers
His love shared through you

Live out your calling
believe you can change the world
All things possible

Be a source of joy
By your words and your actions
Share His grace and peace

Let your light shine bright
Create your heaven on Earth
Through love and service

Your highest purpose
Bringing good into the world
Each and everyday

As you have been blessed
Be a blessing to others
Reflect God's glory

Prayer a wish made
Offered up with hope and faith
By His will and grace

My daily prayer
May His grace and peace be yours
May you know His love

Printed in the United States
by Baker & Taylor Publisher Services